has been associated with the Center of Intercultural Formation doing some fine and much-needed work on the theological evaluation of pastoral activities in Mexico and Panama, and his dynamic lectures on Teilhard and on pastoral themes have stimulated listeners in both countries.

Ivan D. Illich

Executive Director, Center of Intercultural Formation Cuernavaca, Mexico

Introduction

A single problem dominates not only the spiritual and mystical but also the scientific work of Father Pierre Teilhard de Chardin: the relationship between God and the universe. St. Augustine expressed these two supreme realities in the phrase *Deus et anima*, and Cardinal John Henry Newman with "I and my Creator," but Teilhard broadened the perspective to speak of God and the universe. More than just a singular intellectual position, this view is intimately related to Teilhard's temperament and education. His very nature and his vocation to scholarship led him to feel himself a son of the earth and love it intensely. On the other hand, his education and intellectual formation made him deeply aware that he was a son of heaven, and he loved God with all his strength. It is not surprising, then, that all of his scientific-religious labor was carried out as a single pursuit: the quest for the relationship between the two great loves of his life.

The answer was not easily found. Vestiges of Manicheism, unwittingly reinforced by the Jansenism in vogue during the late nineteenth and the early twentieth centuries, persisted in maintaining an irreducible opposition between matter and spirit, between God and the universe, and epistemologically speaking, between science and faith. "All that is not God is nothing and should be disdained as if it did not exist," a counsel of *The Imitation of Christ*, betrays the same recurrent dualism. Would Teilhard be able to escape this same pseudo-spirituality in his own time? As a novice in Jersey he decided to abandon forever his vocation as a scholar, close his ears to the invitation of the earth, and dedicate himself completely to God: he could see no way to reconcile his two seemingly discordant loves.

The unwarranted limitation imposed by this decision, however, was uncovered and uprooted by the providential intervention of his novice-master, a man far ahead of the spirit of the age. In order to love God, counselled his superior, the young Teilhard had no reason to abandon the world or bid farewell to science. A new dawn thus appeared in the soul of the future scholar. Following as it did a dark night spent in authentic religious struggle, that decisive day might be compared in meaning and grandeur to that which followed Luther's experience in the tower. For the Jesuit, as for Martin Luther, it marked the beginning of a varied and dramatic effort aimed at bringing into accord his loves for God and the universe. As he himself relates:

I couldn't help thinking of the abyss that divides the

intellectual world I was in and whose language I knew, from the theological world of Rome with whose idiom I am also familiar. At first it was something of a shock to realise that the latter could, and indeed must be, just as real as the former; and then I told myself that now perhaps I was capable of so using the first language as to make it fairly express what the other contains but puts into words that most people can no longer understand.[1]

Teilhard may have thought that it was only a new vocabulary that he was going to offer to theology, but what he actually gave was a new Weltanschauung, a vision of a moving world, a view opposed to the Ptolemaic description of a static and completed cosmos. The first appearance of Teilhard's revolutionary view took the form of a phenomenology of the cosmos which he developed in just three chapters. At the opening of the work he faithfully describes the universe—its component parts and the whole—and reaches the conclusion that the world evolves; in the second chapter he determines that the direction of evolution is convergent, and in the third he takes a stand with regard to the future. Still hypothetically, but with great assurance and an abundance of detail, he attests to the slow gestation of a superorganism which, bringing with it all the acquisitions of evolution, is gradually centering on a personal, present, autonomous, and transcendent point called Omega. This superorganism is the universe in which we exist and move. To be convinced of all this, to live it as Teilhard did, constitutes the "cosmic sense" which dominated his spirit and which he defines as "the more or less clear affinity which links us psychologically to the whole which envelops us."[2]

With his "cosmic sense" thus clarified, he faithfully pursued his deepening intuition by paying heed to a tendency within himself which he called the "Christic sense," the inclination of the Christian to see the center and end of all things in Christ. St. Paul has given the best insight into the Christic sense of the world. According to the apostle, Christ will be the center and head of all creation. The entire cosmos awaits the new order in which the Son will be lord of the universe, gathering all the saved to himself in one body to deliver them up to the Father.[3]

With its demonstration beginning from the phenomenology of the cosmos, this Christic sense was Father Teilhard's most profound conviction. For the world to achieve perfection, in order that evolution *non sit frustra*, in fact even for evolution to be possible at the level of thought, it was necessary for God to partially immerse himself in matter and become an element of the earth. The essence of Teilhard's work can be summed up in these words: God had to become incarnate and die on the cross. O. A. Rabut is correct in affirming that the religious work of Teilhard de Chardin is nothing more nor less than a synthesis of St. Paul and evolution.[4] Christ himself is the Omega point postulated by evolution. He is, therefore, the author of evolution and the focal point which polarizes the evolutionary process.[5]

All of this applies mainly to the historical Christ, but the Jesus of history is nevertheless only the beginning. Christ, considered in his total dimension, has still not been completely formed. It is human endeavor, representing in turn all the effort of the earth, which must complete him. For this reason matter is "holy matter" and human effort "the very marrow of the universe."[6]

How "a reconciliation is possible between cosmic love for the world and supernatural love for God, . . . between the cult of progress and the yearning for God's love,"[7] now becomes apparent. The point of encounter between God and the world, the place where the two realities are joined in embrace, is Christ. That is why at the end of his prodigious and fruitful labor Teilhard came to the conclusion that "it is only the science of Christ running through all things . . . that really matters."[8] For the same reason his greatest aspiration was to be the evangelist of Christ in the universe. Like St. Paul he desired to know nothing but Christ Crucified. As N. M. Wildiers says, "All of creation appears to him in relation to the Incarnate Word."[9]

Christ and the world appear to Teilhard so intimately and physically conjoined that it is impossible to plunge into the science of the cosmos without passing naturally and spontaneously to the Jesus of the Gospel. Conversely, it is equally impossible to believe in the Jesus of the Gospel without venturing into the science of the cosmos. Thus it is that at the level of human experience Christ and the universe come to be two articles of a single creed. On April 7, 1955, only three days before his death, anxious to fuse his experience as scientist and believer into a single formula, Teilhard wrote in his diary: "The two articles of my Credo: The Universe is centrated—Evolutively (Upward and Forward); Christ is its Centre."[10] It would be difficult to find a more felicitous expression of the relationship between God and the cosmos.

Confronted with the great Teilhardian synthesis, many accuse its author of oversimplifying the reconciliation of science and faith. Paul Chauchard maintains that this accusation is "the most beautiful tribute paid to Teilhard because this apparent ease was the arduous and crucifying endeavor of a lifetime."[11] It would have been easier to divide his life into two compartments: to be a good paleontologist like so many others and, apart from that, a model Jesuit. He would not have scandalized the scientists by behaving as a believer as well as a scholar; nor would he have scandalized many believers by integrating the faith with a seeming scientific materialism which has so often been used to undermine it. But this unnatural separation was not in keeping with his vocation as scientist-priest. He assumed the responsibility of all precursors and bore the cross of every prophet. Father Leroy speaks of the anguish which Teilhard de Chardin experienced because he was not understood. Yet despite the interpretation of the Marxist Kahane, Teilhard was not disheartened by any suspicion of inconsistency in his personal synthesis. What did disturb him, however, was finding himself alone in seeing these things as evident, and at the same time not being able to dialogue fruitfully with either the philosophers or the theologians. He suffered the agony of solitude, but he did not give up. If they did not understand him then, they would one day. He himself said, "It is sufficient that the truth appear but once in one spirit for nothing ever again to be able to stop presence of consciousness in the universe? Of course consciousness is not immediately discernible in the *within* of matter, but it can be perceived indirectly by keeping in mind the fundamental unity of the cosmos, unity by reason of which "a phenomenon necessarily has an omnipresent value and roots."[10] If consciousness is an observable phenomenon in man, it cannot occur in isolation. On the contrary, "it has a cosmic extension, and as such is surrounded by an aura of indefinite spatial and temporal extensions."[11] There are varying degrees of consciousness; in stone it is less perfect than in man. Consciousness, then, appears "as a cosmic property of variable size."[12]

Because of its importance in the subsequent development of his thought, Teilhard's concept of consciousness requires being probed somewhat more deeply. Consciousness is, as Claude Cuénot explains:

> every form of psychic manifestation, from the weakest and most elementary to the most concentrated and highly reflective. It is the specific property of the perfected states of matter, but it would never have appeared had it not been prepared for from the beginning in the very stuff of the universe.[13]

Consciousness is synonymous with centro-complexity and is the coefficient which determines the degree of centration (soul) and of complexity (body and especially brain), centration itself being directly related to complexity. The greater the centration, the greater the complexity; the greater the complexity, the greater the consciousness. While the centration of elements shows the degree of complexity of the whole, it is the complexity of the whole which reveals the

5

level of consciousness. But it is also the level of consciousness which manifests the greater or lesser complexity of the being which possesses it and, consequently, the greater or lesser degree of "being."

The preceding description reveals the nature of radial energy. Because of it, not only life but also psychic activity and consciousness have omnipresent value and roots. But beyond that, radial energy infuses into the cosmos "a universal will to live [which] converges and is hominised in [man]."[14] Thus it is radial energy which *animates and impels evolution.*

Discovered in the nineteenth century, evolution is the crucial category of Teilhardian thought. Teilhard discovered very early that it extended throughout the totality of the spatio-temporal phenomenon. "It was during my studies at Hastings," he writes, "when, little by little—much less as an abstract notion than as a *presence*—the consciousness of a profound, ontological, total drift of the universe around me began to take form, until finally it completely pervaded my interior horizon."[15] For him the awareness of time, that is, of the evolutionary nature of reality, is the fundamental revolution which has affected our vision of the world since a century ago.

Evolution essentially means that the universe is a temporal phenomenon: it is being born around us; it is being created and is not yet completed. For millions and millions of years the universe has been being formed in an uninterrupted process of cosmogenesis, in a slow and painful gestation.

This naturally implies "a *physical bond* among liv-

The Structure
of the Cosmos

For Teilhard de Chardin the cosmos is a kind
of "gigantic atom"[1] with a double aspect,[2]
charged with two forces or energies: tangential energy
which traverses the *without* of things and radial energy which traverses the *within*.

Tangential energy (that energy by which a knife
cuts or an acid dissolves metal) is governed by the
law of entropy, which implies two consequences. The
first is the irreversible disintegration of energy into
heat: "The more the energy-quantum of the world
comes into play, the more it is consumed."[3] Secondly,
it implies the tendency of the universe toward an
equilibrium of energy and ultimately a static condition. If we consider only tangential energy, it would
seem that the concrete, material universe will be un-
able to continue its advance indefinitely. "This path
leads us only to the uninhabited wastelands of lunar
landscapes."[4]

Since tangential energy by itself is thus insufficient to explain the advancing of evolution, it is necessary to resort to another factor: radial energy. Teilhard describes it in two ways. First of all, it is that which "draws it [the element] towards ever greater complexity and centricity—in other words forwards."[5] Secondly and more precisely, radial energy is that *psychic energy* (in man, spiritual energy) "which acts directly between consciousness and consciousness and is manifested at the human level as psychological phenomena."[6] From these two definitions it can be concluded that radial energy is of a psychic nature and that its function is to give impetus to evolution.

Teilhard supports his conviction of the psychic nature of radial energy on the basis of the principle that nothing can appear in the cosmos unless it has always been in preparation. *"Nothing could ever burst forth as final across the different thresholds successively traversed by evolution (however critical they might be) which has not already existed in an obscure and primordial way."*[7] If life exists today, it is because it was being prepared from all time. *"In a coherent perspective of the world: life inevitably assumes a 'pre-life' for as far back before it as the eye can see."*[8] At its highest levels, life is endowed with psychic properties, and the aforementioned principle indicates that even psychic life resides rudimentarily in the more elementary states of matter. Similarly, the "dead" proteins "would be incomprehensible if they did not possess already, deep down in themselves, some sort of rudimentary psyche."[9] Does not this "panpsychicism," correctly understood, point in turn to the omni-

4

ing things"[16] which organically determines the appearance of each. Neither man nor horse nor the first cell could have appeared earlier or later than they did. There is "an immense bond in the becoming" of the world.[17]

As Claude Tresmontant observes: "The scientific concept of evolution is the phenomenological reverse of the metaphysical concept of creation. Scientifically, starting from reality, we verify the fact that the universe is not 'a thing put there,' but a series of things being created one from another."[18] Those who oppose the metaphysical notion of creation to the scientific idea of evolution make two lamentable errors. In the first place, they assume without justification that creation must be an instantaneous act; secondly, they think that evolution is ontologically autonomous, even though it is not the task of science to decide whether it is or not. Science limits itself to establishing the facts and leaves to metaphysics the discovery of the ultimate cause of the evolutionary process.

In summary, evolution is "the expression of the structural law (both of being and of knowledge) by reason of which *nothing, absolutely nothing,* could exist in our lives and visions except by being born; it is, in other words, synonymous with the spatio-temporal pan-interconnection of the phenomenon."[19] Evolution, however, should not be identified with a specific transformistic theory, such as Darwinism or Lamarckism. Being an evolutionist does not mean believing that living things literally descend from each other by the process of generation; nor does it imply an avowal of atheism or materialism.[20] We must

7

understand this: Teilhard de Chardin repeatedly and urgently demands, in order to approach the thesis of evolution with less suspicion and greater interest, a sincerely determined effort to utilize its conclusions for a renewal of theology.

Essentially evolution is not a hypothesis but rather a general method of investigation accepted on a practical level by all scientists. It is a form of knowledge—historical knowledge—extended to zoology and botany.[21]

2

The Direction of Evolution

All scholars now accept the fact of evolution, but not all agree that evolution has a certain orientation, a direction. Many relegate this question to the domain of metaphysics.

Nevertheless, modern psychology has shown that an integral scientific phenomenology does not exclude, but rather includes, the determination of the orientation of a given phenomenon.[1] The scientific study of a phenomenon is in itself a search for its orientation.

The great originality of Teilhard lies precisely in his having found a direction in evolution. He is quite certain that science, though it has not yet reached a decision, is implicitly and completely "already oriented toward the recognition and admission of directed cosmogenesis."[2] He therefore devoted himself to the search for a law of recurrence which would define and measure the development of the "cosmic stuff" throughout time. The result was the law of com-

9

plexity-consciousness: throughout the course of time, matter has been oriented "towards more and more complex states."[3]

What does Teilhard mean by *complexity?* Clarification of the concept demands that it be carefully distinguished from heterogeneity. If we set in order the 360 types of atomic nuclei known to today's physicists, the result would not be a complex grouping but a heterogeneous one, an aggregate. In other words, the number and the variety of elements are sufficient factors to determine a heterogeneous grouping. For complexity, however, something more is required, namely organization, and this results in an "interiorization" of the whole.[4] Thus, true complexity is not defined "solely by the number and variety of elements which constitute the whole,"[5] for it also demands organization, centralization, or interiority to establish multiple links among the elements.[6]

Tresmontant points out three advantages of the law of complexity:

1) It allows natural and genetic classification of the material realities which have appeared in the course of time. Everything from the atom to the highest living being has its place in the classification table, a place which dates each element, i.e. situates each chronologically in time.[7]

2) The law of complexity terminates the long-standing opposition between physics and biology by replacing it with an ascending continuum. There are not two series but a single one which becomes increasingly more complex with time. "The Universe organises itself in a single, grand progression, somewhat

untidy no doubt, but on the whole clear in its orientation, ascending from the most rudimentary atom to the highest form of living things."[8]

3) From a philosophical point of view the law of complexity frees us from the ancient opposition between the one and the many.

> There is really no antinomy between the one and the many if things are seen as subsisting in a continuum of personalization; they are merely two phases (or more precisely two directions) of the same reality which surrounds us. Spirit and matter are contradictory if they are isolated or symbolized as abstract, fixed, and therefore impossible notions—as pure plurality and pure simplicity. *In natura rerum* one is inseparable from the other because the one essentially follows upon a synthesis of the other.[9]

The law of complexity supposes real continuity between matter and life, matter and consciousness, matter and spirit. In a fixed and static view of the universe these two realities are inexplicably connected in a purely verbal manner; in an evolutionary perspective, however, thanks to the law of complexity there is a necessary union between the two orders of matter and spirit. Because the growing complexity of matter is directed through interiorization toward an ever more obvious presence of consciousness in the universe, the law expressing it is called the law of complexity-consciousness. It is this law which permits the natural progression from simple cosmogenesis to biogenesis, from biogenesis to anthropogenesis, and from anthropogenesis to the genesis of the suprahuman.

11

Contents

Contents

it from invading and inflaming everything."[12]

I cannot disguise my apprehension at undertaking the arduous task of interpreting Teilhard. So much has been written so magnificently about his work. My intention is less to write an exegesis of the work of the French scholar than to point out the lightly-sketched guideposts he left on the path toward christological renewal. Christology has been practically stationary since the Council of Chalcedon, and there is much talk of the need for its revival as the basis of the renewal of ecclesiology and the pastoral action of the People of God. But few have seen the vast possibilities which the Teilhardian vision offers in this area, perhaps because his complete works have not yet been published or because there is as yet no critical edition of them; perhaps also because the "Teilhard phenomenon" is still at an intensely controversial stage, or because there remains some fear of the doctrine of evolution which has changed the interpretation of the universe; perhaps, too, because we are still at the fringe of scientific progress—whatever the reason, the work of integrating Teilhardian thought with revealed doctrine has barely begun.

Neither unaware of the difficulty of the task nor oblivious to the risks implied, I believe that it is the obligation of theologians to take much more seriously the testimony of a man who lived entirely for Christ and knew better than any of them the secrets of the universe. Let them analyze, criticize, purify—but let them also assimilate what can be assimilated. There is much and it is precious. They will not be able to do it alone. I agree with Rabut when he says, "It is very probable that only the work of a team including, as a minimum, a real scientist, a real philosopher, and a real theologian will be able to shed sufficient light on the difficult questions which Teilhard has attacked so confidently and almost ingenuously."[13] For my part, I aspire to facilitate in some way the work of the true theologian.

Francisco Bravo

PART I

The Phenomenology of the Cosmos

Father Teilhard de Chardin's contribution to Christology is the revelation of the place and function of Christ in an evolutively centrated universe. This he does with remarkable consistency and an exceptional sense of the whole. Of course the task depends on a prior description of the cosmos—its evolving structure, the direction of evolution, the future of the universe —in short, a phenomenology of the cosmos. The first part of this study, therefore, will be an attempt to explain Teilhard's phenomenology of the cosmos by examining in detail the first article of the Teilhardian creed: "The Universe is evolutively centrated."

The Future
of the Universe

Since it is beyond the scope of this study to trace step by step the history of the world, which is really no different from the history of the increasing complexity of matter, let us enter it at the critical point of most interest to us: the appearance of thought.

The principal result of the appearance of thought in the universe is reflection. Through it man obtains insight into the future and the task of self-evolution toward ever more perfected states. Reflection thus becomes "the key to evolution,"[1] for it not only explains the past but reveals the future.

During the nineteenth and early twentieth centuries scientists were mainly concerned with clarifying man's past. Their investigations established that the appearance of thought corresponded biologically to a "hominization" of life. But today, with scientific research directed toward the future, an even more astonishing outlook is taking form: "that of the progressive humanization of mankind."² Here Teilhard poses a new problem which is the subject of this chapter.

In the past the whole cosmos moved not only *localiter* but *entitative*, since it was continuously acquiring more being and, consequently, a progressive change in its nature. But is this process still progressively advancing? Teilhard replies in the affirmative. The manner and direction of this movement, then, must be sought.

The Three Alternatives

Three pairs of alternatives are open to us in considering the progress of the world toward the future: pessimism or optimism, the optimism of withdrawal or the optimism of evolution, convergent or divergent evolution.

The first option is a response to the problem "to be or not to be." Which is better? Which is more worthy of being chosen? Matter has already decided that it is better to be than not to be, and hence it has always been directed toward higher forms of being. Man represents the highest degree of being as yet achieved by nature.

Having the optimistic side, let us consider, then, the second set of alternatives: the optimism of withdrawal or the optimism of evolution. Man must decide at this point whether to remain where he is or to keep on going. Some deny all meaning, value, and progress to being. Such thinkers, needless to say, flatly reject the advance to the end. They evade the question in quietism, in "What does it matter?" and "Who cares?" They believe that the highest state of being exists here and now and they try to exploit it to the fullest by abandoning themselves to pleasure or, like the Buddhists, by turning to mysticism.[3] Others, however, believe in the possibility of an even more highly developed consciousness, and they choose to go on to the end along the path of evolution. Obviously Teilhard is among them.

The decision having been made to proceed to the end, the choice of path now assumes importance. The question of how to reach the ultimate end gives rise to the third pair of alternatives. Two paths are open: plurality or unity, convergence toward a central part or divergence.

Bergson chose the plurality and divergence. According to the Jewish philosopher, the world is evolving toward dispersal. As it advances, its elements acquire greater autonomy. Each being is to achieve its own utmost originality and its maximum freedom in opposition to all the others. Perfection, bliss, and supreme grandeur belong to the part, not to the whole. From this dispersive point of view, socialization of the human masses seems to be absurd regression or servitude. "Essentially . . . the Universe spreads like a fan: it is *divergent* in structure."[4]

Teilhard stands counter to Bergson on this issue. According to Teilhard, nothing exists nor ultimately matters but the whole. It would be a grave error for an element of the world to become self-absorbed and separated from the others, to egoistically isolate itself. "Essentially the Universe is narrowing to a centre, like

15

the successive layers of a cone: it is *convergent* in structure."[5]

Proof of Teilhard's position requires turning again to the law of complexity-consciousness, through which is discovered "the growth, within and around us, of a greater awareness."[6] But greater awareness can only occur on the basis of greater *union*. In effect, greater awareness is equivalent to a higher level of being, and "fuller being is closer union."[7] Consequently a greater degree of awareness means a higher level of being, and a higher level of being means greater union.

Because of this conviction Teilhard severely criticizes Bergson's position:

> To adopt the hypothesis of a *final* divergence of Life is, in fact, to introduce biologically into the thinking part of the world an immediate principle of disintegration and death. It is to re-establish, at the very antipodes of Consciousness (become no more than a fleeting reality!), the primacy and preponderant stability of Matter.[8]

Socialization and Superorganism

The choices being made, it is now necessary to name the process which evolution pursues at the level of thought. Teilhard calls it *socialization*. The evolutionary process which originated in multiplicity and reached individualization in man is now directed toward socialization.[9] Is it not clear, Teilhard asks, that mankind has made astonishing advances in organization during the last twenty to twenty-five thousand years (since the Age of the Reindeer)? Economic organization: the unification of the energies of the

16

earth; intellectual organization: the unification of knowledge into a coherent system (science); social organization: the unification of the human masses into a thinking whole.[10]

The collective march of mankind persistently proceeds, but toward what? Toward something which Teilhard, relating it to man as he now is, calls *ultrahumanity*, the ultra-human, or the superorganism. This is not to be confused with Nietzsche's superman, who is the personification of inhuman individualism and more properly corresponds to the conclusion of a process of divergent evolution. Teilhard's ultra-humanity represents a higher collective critical point which will lead in time to a true *superorganism* formed by a conciliation of individuals, just as the body can be said to be a conciliation of cells.[11] It might more aptly be called a *superperson*.

Superorganism and the Law of Union

Does not this superorganism or superperson threaten to absorb and annihilate the individual? Is Bergson right in saying that socialization is regression? Does not defense of socialization support Marxism at its most indefensible point, i.e. in its lack of esteem for the person? Teilhard reacts against one of our most deeply-rooted prejudices: the tendency to set up an opposition between plurality and unity, part and whole, individuality and collectivity. Such a dichotomy paves the way for a monistic destiny leading to a superperson which would indeed exact the sacrifice and bring about the destruction of personal values in the universe. This is an unfortunate confusion of association and agglomeration. There is no doubt that agglomeration suffocates and neutralizes the elements involved. But "superorganism" refers to an association. Thus:

> Alongside these massive inorganic groupings in which the elements intermingle and drown, or more exactly at the opposite pole to them, Nature shows herself to be full of associations brought about and organically ordered by a precisely opposite law. In the case of associations of this kind (the only true and natural associations) the coming together of the separate elements does nothing to eliminate their differences. On the contrary, *it exalts them*. In every practical sphere *true union* (that is to say, synthesis) does not confound; it differentiates.[12]

But merely affirming this is insufficient; it must be proven. Teilhard does so with recourse to the law of union. Referring to the beings subject to it, the law states: "The more 'other' they become in conjunction, the more they find themselves as 'self.'"[13] This is apparent with friends and with lovers who discover the depths of their own hearts and minds only in communication with each other. Union, then, has "a *function of personalisation*,"[14] and the same thing that occurs between two persons occurs with the whole of humanity.

> By virtue of the emergence of Thought a special and novel environment has been evolved among human individuals within which they acquire the faculty of associating together, and reacting upon one another, no longer primarily for the preservation and continuance of the species but for the creation of a common consciousness.[15]

18

Thus socialization, whose hour seems to have come for humanity, by no means signifies "the ending of the Era of the Individual upon earth, but far more its beginning."[16] The element "only becomes personal when it universalises itself,"[17] and conversely, it can truly universalize itself only through personalization. It would be a great mistake to accuse Teilhard of minimizing the dignity and value of the human person. According to Ligneul, he ranks with Emmanuel Mounier among the great representatives of personalism.[18] Mounier teaches that "every doctrine, every civilization which affirms the primacy of the human person over material needs and the collective apparatus which sustains his development is personalistic." Teilhard does just this. Furthermore, going beyond all the concepts of his predecessors, he makes the person the center of reference for scientific thought and sees that absolutely everything in the world is for man, who is in turn for Jesus Christ. As progress continues, there will be increasing union among men and with it an ever clearer common consciousness, which is what will ultimately constitute an ultra-humanity.

Collectivism and Personalism

Teilhard goes on to examine the conditions for the acquisition of this common consciousness which is the formal cause of the ultra-human. Here again he suggests two solutions: the collectivist and his own, the personalist.

Collectivism is content that the human elements follow the law of union: that they relate to each other

19

in a sort of closed circuit in which each thinking monad intellectually and affectively links itself to each of the others, and reaches a maximum of individual dominion by sharing in a certain ultimate clarity of vision and warmth of sympathy. A superior state of consciousness diffused through the ultra-technified, ultra-socialized, ultra-cerebralized layers of the human mass, but without the appearance (neither necessary nor conceivable) of any universal, defined, or autonomous center of reflection within the system: this is what is foreseen and aspired to at the upper limit of hominization in the collectivist hypothesis.[19]

Personalism, on the other hand, postulates and foresees a *center of union* at the top of the structure.

> To fuse together the human multitude . . . without crushing it, it seems essential that there should be a field of attraction at once powerful and irreversible, and such as cannot emanate collectively from a simple nebula of reflecting atoms, but which requires as its source a self-subsisting, strongly personalised star.[20]

Obviously, in demanding the existence of a centralized star, Teilhard leaves the realm of science and, by conscious extrapolation, moves into the terrain of hyperphysics. But this does not prevent his enthusiastic proclamation that the very success of evolution consists in the existence and discovery of this star which is not *Something* but *Someone*,[21] a person, a real "I" at the summit of the world. "A veritable *Ego* at the summit of the world is needed for the consummation, without confounding them, of all the elemental *egos* of Earth."[22]

20

The Omega Point

Although he knows that the star is Someone, Teilhard is still unaware of who he is; nor does he know his name. For the moment he designates him with an algebraic sign. He calls him the *Omega point*.

The function proper to Omega is to add up and accumulate the store of consciousness which has developed little by little on the earth through noogenesis.[23] By "adding up consciousness" the disciples of Marx mean the gathering together of human achievements (ideas, discoveries, artistic creations, etc.); these could be considered radii of consciousness. Teilhard cannot accept the Marxist explanation, however, for a sum of radii is not enough. What must be gathered are the centers of consciousness. "The very centre of our consciousness, deeper than all its radii; that is the essence which Omega, if it is to be truly Omega, must reclaim."[24] This center is not only our works but our very self; not merely the conscious, but consciousness.

Let us recall again that the common consciousness accumulated in Omega is not a cosmic monster which absorbs and annihilates the individual personality. Rather it is the community of love in which individuals find their personality—a personality which is just barely suggested and outlined at the level of individuality. Teilhard has been frequently and very unjustly accused of exalting social values at the expense of individual ones, but nothing could be further from the truth. What he did was to trace faithfully the successive stages of evolution. When evolution reached the reflective level, it brought a need for man to indi-

21

vidualize himself. By his biological nature, primitive man tends to isolate himself, to retreat inward, to become egoistical. Only when he discovers others and establishes a community of interests with them does he become aware of himself, master of his actions, and capable of giving himself to others. No longer a mere individual, he becomes, not ontologically but existentially, a person. As Mounier puts it, "The person grows only to the extent that he constantly purifies himself of the individual which exists within him."[25] The individual is that which is imperfect and primitive in man. What is perfect is the person, and the person can only develop in association. The person reaches fulfillment not by being concerned for himself but by putting himself at the service of others and therefore becoming more transparent to himself and them. The way to the "I" of each is the "you" of the others.

According to Teilhard the Omega point has autonomy, actuality, irreversibility, and transcendency. If its role is "initiating and maintaining within its radius the unanimity of the world's 'reflective' particles,"[26] it must necessarily be present and real. "A present and real noosphere goes with a real and present centre."[27] If the Omega point is to satisfy the ultimate demands of our action, it "must be independent of the collapse of the forces with which evolution is woven";[28] it must be irreversible. These attributes permit Omega to transcend temporal and spatial limitations: "If by its very nature it did not escape from the time and space which it gathers together, it would not be Omega."[29]

22

It would be superfluous to add that a subject with such attributes is autonomous.

Love

The centration of the thinking monads around Omega occurs not through simple reflection but mainly through "conspiracy." Before men can be united in a common consciousness, a preliminary stage which Teilhard calls "conciliation of individuals" must take place.

> "Conspiracy," the origin of the utterly new kind of union which distinguishes the human layer from all the other forms of terrestrial life, is the ability of the various consciousnesses taken as a whole to unite (through language and a thousand other more obscure bonds) to constitute a great whole in which, in a reflective way, each element is aware of its grouping with the others.[30]

This "conspiracy" is not induced from outside the thinking monads; it comes from within through love. The individuals' entrance into the superorganism "should not take the form of a functional and enforced mechanisation of human energies (the totalitarian principle), but of a 'conspiracy' informed with love."[31] Teilhard regrets that love has always been carefully separated from the realistic and positivistic concepts of the world. One day we shall have to recognize it as the basic energy of life, the only natural means by which the ascending movement of evolution can continue. Without love we are faced with the prospect of standardization and slavery, the fate of the termite and the ant. Within and through love we will

23

find the deepening of our innermost self in life-giving human communication, the free and fanciful rise of the spirit over all unexplored paths.

> It links those who love in bonds that unite but do not confound, causing them to discover in their mutual contact an exaltation capable, incomparably more than any arrogance of solitude, of arousing in the heart of their being all that they possess of uniqueness and creative power.[32]

Teilhard is not referring to the sentimental aspect of love, to the delights and joys it causes. For his purposes he prefers to examine its natural dynamism and its evolutionary significance. Love as the affinity of being for being—it is this aspect which contributes to determining the ultimate stages of the human phenomenon.

Love exists at three levels: it is a property of matter, of life, and of man. As a property of matter it is none other than the "natural love" described by the scholastics. It has always existed, and we could say that it is a necessary condition for love at the level of life and thought. "If there were no internal propensity to unite, even at a prodigiously rudimentary level—indeed in the molecule itself—it would be physically impossible for love to appear higher up, with us, in 'hominised' form."[33] At all three levels love is nothing other than the more or less direct trace drawn in the element's heart by the psychic convergence of the universe on itself.

Permeation of self and permeation of everything with an absolute and personal love is the supreme means of converging toward the center of centers, toward Omega which is the great love. We have already seen that evolution is an increase in complexity. Teilhard goes even further and affirms that this increase in complexity is an increase in love.[34]

In accordance with our considerations in this chapter, Chauchard observes that man is a social species. In social beings a new level of love appears: the need for others, the fact that the solitary individual cannot find his proper balance, and that his life can become impossible without it. Man is only normal and natural in a natural society—a society in which there is a balance between the need for others and the need for individual growth, between self-love and the love of others. If at the animal level love is instinctive, in man it is a duty. The prophet of a superhumanity, Teilhard speaks of a superlove, a universal love, an "agaposphere" synonymous with the noosphere.

Teilhard has often been unjustly accused of being an optimist who ignores what is bad. He was perfectly aware that, despite all theoretical predictions and our own hopes, modern attempts at human collectivization have led only to diminution and slavery of consciousnesses, making of man a mere number or a cog in a machine. But what has been the basis of these attempts at union? Fundamentally, self-interest. It is not strange, then, that this leads to man's mechanization. "Love alone is capable of uniting living beings in such a way as to complete and fulfil them, for it alone takes them and joins them by what is deepest in themselves. This is a fact of daily experience."[35]

But is universal love possible? Is it not precisely at this point that we invoke the impossible? It seems utopian to expect love on a universal scale. First of all, man is extremely limited; he can affect at best a

25

single being or perhaps a few. Beyond this, love ends and cold justice and reason remain. Secondly, "loving everything and everyone" is a false and contradictory gesture which in the end only leads to loving nothing.

Nevertheless Teilhard, who has been called the witness of love, continues to hope for universal love. Human nature cannot go on being frustrated. Certainly hatred and repulsion exist around us, but hate is merely the pathological manifestation of love. We must make a decision so that love can break through and renew the face of the earth. Let us "make up our minds to accept the possibility, indeed the reality, of some *source* of love and *object* of love at the summit of the world above our heads."[36] Collectivity kills love; what is merely collective is essentially unlovable. "Love . . . dies in contact with the impersonal and the anonymous."[37] Only when the universe takes on a face and a heart will we see the blossoming of the basic attractions within the atmosphere created by this focus. Only then, under the imperious pressure provoked by an infolding earth, will burst forth the formidable energies of attraction which lie dormant among human molecules.

> For the failure that threatens us to be turned into success, for the concurrence of human monads to come about, it is necessary and sufficient for us that we should extend our science to its farthest limits and recognise and accept (as being necessary to close and balance space-time) not only some vague future existence, but also . . . the radiation *as a present reality* of that mysterious centre of our centres which I have called Omega.[38]

PART II

The Place and Function of Christ in the Cosmos

In our description of the evolutionary process of the world, we have now reached a point beyond which it is impossible to continue without discovering the overpowering and radiant face of Christ as he takes possession of the universe and assumes the right and duty to lead it on to its ultimate end. Teilhard de Chardin raises the question: what is the place and function of Christ in the world? Before undertaking an answer to this, we must first consider Christ in Teilhard's methodology.